ISABELLA SMITH

Dog Training Bible

A Complete Guide To Raising An Exceptional Dog Through Positive Reinforcement And Mental Exercise From Puppy To Adult

Copyright © 2023 by Isabella Smith

All rights reserved. No part of this publication may be reproduced, stored or transmitted in any form or by any means, electronic, mechanical, photocopying, recording, scanning, or otherwise without written permission from the publisher. It is illegal to copy this book, post it to a website, or distribute it by any other means without permission.

First edition

This book was professionally typeset on Reedsy.
Find out more at reedsy.com

Contents

A FREE GIFT TO OUR READERS	v
Introduction	vii

I Puppy Primer: Understanding Your Furry Friend

1	Understanding Your Puppy	3
2	Puppy-Proofing	10
3	Creating a Safe and Stimulating Environment	15
4	Basic Care and Maintenance	19

II The ABCs of Dog Training: Basic Commands for a Well-Behaved Pup

5	Creating a Positive Learning Environment	29
6	Development Stages	32
7	Training Older Dogs	35
8	Crate Training	40
9	Potty Training	46
10	Basic Commands	53

III Beyond Sit and Stay: Advanced Training and Health Tips for a Happy Dog

11	Advanced Training	61
12	Socialization Training	69

| 13 | Agility Training | 72 |
| 14 | Behavior Modification | 75 |

IV   Mental Exercises For A Sharp Dog

15	Mental Exercise	83
16	Conclusion	91
17	FAQ	94

A FREE GIFT TO OUR READERS

Get your Free Gift here:

Introduction

Dogs have been our friendly companions for thousands of years, and there's no denying the special bond we share with our four-legged friends. As pet owners, we have a great responsibility to ensure that our dogs get the best possible care, and that includes training them properly.

Training your puppy is essential for their well-being and happiness. Not only does it help prevent behavioral issues and ensure their safety, but it also makes the bond between your furry friend and you stronger. However, there are many misconceptions about dog training that can lead to ineffective and even harmful methods.

That's why I wrote the "Dog Training Bible" – a comprehensive guide to training your puppy with effective, humane, and science-based methods. In this book, you'll learn everything you need to know about understanding your puppy's needs, teaching basic and advanced commands, addressing behavioral issues, and more.

It's highly recommended to start training your puppy early on in their life. Puppies are like sponges - they absorb information quickly and are eager to learn. This is why puppyhood is the perfect time to start teaching them good habits and behaviors that will last a lifetime.

Additionally, puppies are generally easier to teach than older dogs. They are more open to new experiences and have fewer ingrained bad habits. This makes it easier to teach them basic obedience, socialization, and other essential skills.

But don't worry if you've missed the early stages of your puppy's life. It's never too late to start training, and many of the techniques outlined in this book can be applied to older dogs as well.

So, whether you have a brand-new puppy or an older dog who needs some training, in this book, you will discover the tools and knowledge you need to create a happy, healthy, and well-behaved canine companion.

The book also covers important topics such as nutrition, exercise, grooming, and health, which are crucial for ensuring that your puppy is healthy and happy. Whether you're a first-time dog owner or a highly experienced trainer, this book has something for everyone.

So, if you want to give your puppy the best possible start in life, join me as we explore the world of puppy training together. Let's create a stronger bond between you and your furry friend and make training a fun and rewarding experience for both of you.

I

Puppy Primer: Understanding Your Furry Friend

1

Understanding Your Puppy

Puppies are not just cuddly and cute; they are complex animals with their own unique behaviors and personalities. To train your puppy effectively, it's important to understand their psychology and needs. This chapter will provide you with a foundation of knowledge about puppies, including how they think and learn, how to establish a bond with them, and how to recognize their basic needs.

Understanding Your Puppy's Psychology

Puppies have their own unique psychology that is shaped by their instincts, behaviors, socialization, and learning abilities. By understanding these aspects of your puppy's psychology, you can train them more effectively and build a stronger bond with them.

I. Instincts and Behaviors

Puppies are born with a set of instincts and behaviors that help them survive in the wild. Understanding these instincts and behaviors can help you train your puppy more effectively. Here are the most common instincts and behaviors:

Pack mentality: Puppies are social animals that instinctively seek out the company of other dogs or humans. This is why they often display separation anxiety when left alone.

Bite inhibition: Puppies learn to control their bite force through play and socialization. Without proper training, this can lead to biting and aggression in adulthood.

Chewing: Puppies chew to relieve teething discomfort and explore their environment. Providing appropriate chew toys can help satisfy this instinct and prevent destructive chewing.

II. Socialization

Socialization is the process by which puppies learn to interact with other dogs and humans. Early socialization is crucial for developing good behavior and preventing aggression. Some key points to keep in mind include:

- Exposing your puppy to a variety of animals, people, and environments during their critical socialization phase (between 3-14 weeks of age).
- Providing positive experiences and rewards during socialization to help your puppy associate new experiences with positive feelings.
- Avoiding negative experiences or punishment during socialization, which can lead to fear and anxiety in your puppy.

III. Learning and Memory

Puppies are capable of learning and retaining information from a very young age. Understanding their learning abilities and memory can help you train them more effectively. Some important factors to consider include:

- Using positive reinforcement (rewards) to train your puppy, as this has been shown to be more effective than punishment.
- Consistency and repetition in training, as puppies need to practice behaviors multiple times to learn them.

- Short training sessions, as puppies have short attention spans and can become easily distracted or overwhelmed.

By understanding your puppy's instincts and behaviors, socialization needs, and learning abilities, you can build a stronger bond with them and train them more effectively.

How to Establish a Bond with Your Puppy

Bringing a puppy home is a joyful and thrilling experience. However, it is also a great responsibility, and establishing a strong bond with your new furry friend is essential for their well-being and happiness. Here is how to establish a bond with your puppy:

Spend Quality Time Together: Spending quality time with your puppy is the best way to build a bond. Play with your puppy, take them for walks, and snuggle with them on the couch. This will help your pup feel loved and develop a sense of trust and security with you.

Positive Reinforcement: This is a powerful tool for bonding with your puppy. Reward your puppy for good behavior with treats, praise, and attention. This will help your puppy associate you with happy experiences and create a stronger bond.

Train Your Puppy: Training your puppy is not only essential for their development but also a great way to establish a bond. Training provides an opportunity for you and your puppy to work together and build a relationship based on trust and communication.

Groom Your Puppy: Grooming your puppy is another great way to establish a bond. Brush your puppy's coat, trim their nails, and give them baths. This will not only keep your puppy healthy and clean but also provide a calming and relaxing experience that can strengthen your bond. In the following chapters, you will discover precise instructions on how to groom your puppy in a way that keeps them comfortable and does not cause them anxiety.

Be Respectful of Your Puppy's Needs: Your puppy has their own unique personality, and it's important to respect their needs and boundaries. Pay attention to your puppy's body language and behavior and respond accordingly. This will help your puppy feel safe and secure in your presence and strengthen your bond.

Be Patient: Building a bond with your puppy takes time and patience. Don't expect to develop a strong bond overnight. Be patient and consistent in your interactions with your puppy, and over time, you will build a strong and lasting bond.

Remember, establishing a bond with your puppy is essential for their well-being. When you strengthen the bond with your puppy, you are not only doing it for yourself, but you are also contributing to their happiness.

Understanding Your Puppy's Needs

Puppies have a range of needs that must be met for them to be happy, healthy, and well-behaved. Let's explore the physical, emotional, and behavioral needs of puppies, and provide tips on how to meet those needs.

Physical Needs

Puppies have a number of physical needs that must be met for them to thrive. The most important physical needs include:

Nutrition: Puppies require a well-balanced and nutritious diet to support their growth and development. Choose a high-quality puppy food that meets their nutritional needs.

Exercise: Puppies need regular exercise to build their muscles, maintain their weight, and expend their energy. Provide your puppy with opportunities to run, play, and explore.

Health Care: Puppies require regular visits to the veterinarian to stay healthy. This includes vaccinations, parasite control, and check-ups.

Emotional Needs

Puppies are social animals that require attention and affection to thrive.

Love and Attention: Puppies need to feel loved and valued by their owners. Spend time cuddling, playing, and interacting with your puppy on a daily basis.

Socialization: As previously mentioned, puppies need to be socialized with other dogs and humans to develop good behavior and prevent aggression.

Security and Comfort: Puppies need a safe and comfortable environment that provides them with a sense of security. Provide your puppy with a cozy bed, safe toys, and a secure home environment.

Behavioral Needs

Lastly, there are behavioral needs that, when fulfilled, will help your puppy develop good behavior and prevent problem behaviors. The most essential behavioral needs include:

Positive Reinforcement: Your puppy stopped barking the moment you used a well-established signal between the two of you, such as the sound of a clicker? This is when using a treat to reinforce good behavior is most effective. Keep using treats and affection to teach your dog what kind of behavior is expected from them and rewarded.

Consistency: Puppies thrive on routine and consistency. Establish clear rules and boundaries and stick to them.

Mental Stimulation: Puppies need mental stimulation to prevent boredom and destructive behavior. Provide your puppy with toys, games, and puzzles that challenge their minds.

By understanding and meeting your puppy's physical, emotional, and behavioral needs, you can help them develop into happy, healthy, and well-behaved dogs. In the next chapter, we'll cover the basics of creating a safe and stimulating environment for your puppy.

2

Puppy-Proofing

Bringing a new puppy home is thrilling, but it can also be tiring and overwhelming, especially when it comes to preparing your house for your new furry friend. To make the transition as smooth as possible, it's important to puppy-proof your home before your puppy arrives. In this chapter, we will discuss how to prepare your house for your puppy.

Living Room:

The living room is often the heart of the home, and it's important to make it a comfortable and safe space for your puppy. To prepare your living room for your new furry friend, follow these steps:

- Remove any valuable or fragile objects from the room or place them out of reach of your puppy.
- Cover any exposed electrical cords with cord covers or move them out of reach of your puppy.
- Provide your puppy with enough chew toys to discourage them from chewing on furniture or other non-toy items.
- Consider investing in a pet gate to block off any areas of the room that are off-limits to your puppy.

Kitchen:

The kitchen is a potential danger zone for puppies, so it's important to take extra precautions to keep your puppy safe while they explore their new surroundings. Here's how to prepare your kitchen for your puppy:

- Store all food, cleaning supplies, and chemicals in cabinets or high

shelves that are out of reach of your puppy.
- Place any trash cans behind closed cabinet doors or in a location that is inaccessible to your puppy.
- Keep all small appliances, such as toasters and blenders, out of reach of your puppy.
- Block off any areas where your puppy could get trapped or stuck, such as behind the refrigerator or under the sink.

Bedroom:

The bedroom is often a comfortable and cozy space where your puppy may want to spend time. To make sure your bedroom is safe for your new furry friend, follow these steps:

- Keep any medications or other potentially harmful items out of reach of your puppy.
- Store any loose cords or chargers in a drawer or out of reach of your puppy.
- Consider keeping your bedroom door closed to prevent your puppy from exploring unsupervised.

Bathroom:

The bathroom is another room in the house that can be potentially dangerous for puppies. To prepare your bathroom for your puppy, take these steps:

- Keep all cleaning supplies and chemicals in a cabinet or on a high shelf that your puppy cannot reach.
- Keep toilet lids closed to prevent your puppy from drinking from the toilet or falling in.
- Keep all small items, such as jewelry or hair accessories, out of reach of your puppy.
- Make sure your bathroom door is closed when you're not using it to prevent your puppy from exploring unsupervised.

Backyard:

If you have a backyard, it's important to make sure it's a safe and secure space for your puppy to play and explore. Here's how to prepare your backyard for your new furry friend:

- Make sure your fence is secure and there are no gaps or holes where your puppy could escape.
- Remove any potentially hazardous items from the yard, such as sharp objects or toxic plants.
- Provide your puppy with toys and a comfortable outdoor space to relax in.
- Keep an eye on your puppy while they're outside to ensure their safety.

By following these tips, you can prepare your house for your new puppy and create a safe and comfortable environment for them to explore and play in. Remember, puppy-proofing is an ongoing process, and as your puppy grows and learns, you may need to make adjustments to keep them safe and happy.

3

Creating a Safe and Stimulating Environment

When bringing a new puppy home, it is important to provide them with a safe and comfortable environment.

Comfortable sleeping arrangements: A comfortable and safe sleeping area is crucial for a puppy's physical and emotional well-being. This can include providing a cozy dog bed or crate, using a firm mattress and clean bedding, and keeping the sleeping area free of any hazards.

Cleanliness: A clean home is not only important for hygiene reasons but can also provide a sense of calm and order for the puppy. This includes regularly cleaning and disinfecting surfaces, toys, and other objects the puppy comes into contact with.

Providing stimulation

In addition to a safe and comfortable home, providing toys and other forms of stimulation is important for a puppy's development:

Chew toys: Puppies love to chew, and getting them appropriate chew toys can help prevent destructive chewing on furniture or other household items. Look for toys that are durable, safe, and appropriate for your puppy's size and age.

Interactive toys: Interactive toys, such as puzzle toys or toys that dispense treats, can help keep your puppy mentally stimulated and prevent boredom.

Socialization: Socialization is a critical part of a puppy's development, and providing opportunities for your puppy to interact with other dogs and people can help prevent behavioral problems down the road.

Creating a Routine

Establishing a routine is important for a puppy's physical and emotional well-being. Here is what you should keep in mind when creating a routine:

Feeding schedule: Puppies need to eat frequently throughout the day, and establishing a consistent feeding schedule can help regulate their digestion and prevent accidents in the house.

Exercise routine: Puppies have a lot of energy and need plenty of opportunities to exercise and play. Establishing a routine for walks, playtime, and other forms of exercise can help keep your puppy healthy and happy.

Training sessions: Training your puppy is an important part of their development, and establishing a routine for training sessions can help your puppy learn and grow in a consistent manner.

Having a consistent schedule can help your puppy feel safe, secure, and confident in their environment.

Determine Your Puppy's Needs: Before creating a routine, it's important to understand your puppy's needs. Puppies have different needs than adult dogs, and their routines should reflect this. Consider your puppy's age, breed, energy level, and health status when creating their routine.

Create a Schedule: Once you have determined your puppy's needs, create a schedule that includes regular feeding times, potty breaks, playtime, training sessions, and nap times. Puppies need to eat frequently, so plan to feed your puppy 3-4 times per day. Schedule potty breaks after meals, after naps, and every few hours during the day. Puppies also need plenty of playtime and exercise, so schedule play sessions and walks throughout the day.

Be Consistent: Consistency is key when creating a routine for your puppy. Stick to a consistent schedule every day, including on weekends and holidays. This will make your puppy understand what is expected of them and feel more secure in their environment.

Use positive reinforcement to teach your puppy to follow their routine. Reward your puppy with praise, treats, and attention when they eat, potty outside, play nicely, and follow basic commands. This will help your puppy associate their routine with positive experiences and make them more likely to follow it.

Adjust as Needed: Your puppy's needs will change as they grow and develop. Be prepared to adjust their routine as needed to accommodate their changing needs. For example, as your puppy gets older, they may need fewer potty breaks and more exercise.

By following these tips for creating a safe and stimulating environment for your puppy, you can help ensure that they grow up healthy, happy, and well-adjusted.

4

Basic Care and Maintenance

Taking care of your pet's basic needs is essential for their health and happiness. In this chapter, we'll cover the basics of pet care, including feeding and watering, grooming, and health care.

Feeding and Watering

Feeding your pet a healthy and balanced diet is crucial for their overall well-being. Here are some tips for feeding and watering your pet:

Choose a High-Quality Diet: Select a high-quality diet that meets your pet's nutritional needs. Consult with your veterinarian to determine the best diet for your pet's age, breed, and activity level.

Measure Portions: Overfeeding your pet can lead to obesity and other health problems. Measure out your pet's food portions based on their weight and activity level. Feed your pet on a regular schedule to help them maintain a healthy weight.

Provide Fresh Water: Always provide your pet with fresh, clean water. Change your pet's water daily and ensure they have access to water at all times.

Grooming

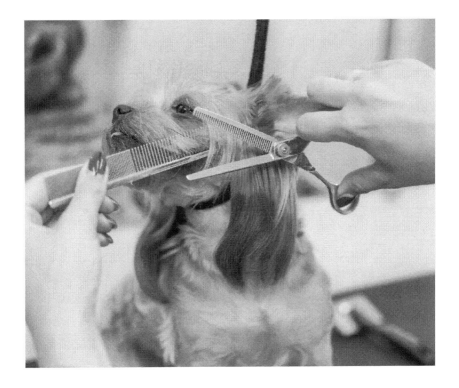

Grooming your puppy is an essential part of their care routine. It not only helps to keep them clean and healthy, but it also makes the bond between you and your furry friend stronger. In this chapter, we will cover the step-by-step instructions for grooming your puppy, including how to bathe them, clean their ears, and more.

Brushing

Brushing your puppy's fur is an essential part of their grooming routine. It helps to remove loose fur, dirt, and debris from their coat, and it also promotes healthy skin and fur growth.

Step 1: Choose the right brush for your puppy's coat type. There are different types of brushes available, including slicker brushes, bristle brushes, and combs.

Step 2: Start by brushing your puppy's fur in the direction of hair growth. Use gentle strokes and be careful not to tug or pull on their fur.

Step 3: Work in sections, starting from the top of their head and working your way down to their tail.

Step 4: Be sure to brush their undercoat as well, as this is where a lot of loose fur and debris can accumulate.

Bathing

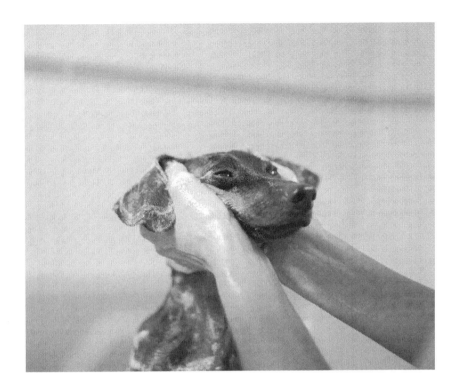

Bathing your puppy is another important part of their grooming routine. It helps to keep their skin and coat clean, and it can also help to prevent skin irritations and infections.

Step 1: Fill a sink or a tub with warm water. Ensure that the water is not too hot or too cold.

Step 2: Wet your puppy's fur with the water, starting from their head and working your way down to their tail.

Step 3: Apply a mild puppy shampoo to the fur of your pup, and work it into a lather.

Step 4: Rinse their fur thoroughly with warm water, making sure to remove all of the shampoo.

Step 5: Use a towel to gently dry your puppy's fur. Be sure to avoid rubbing their fur too hard, as this can cause tangling or matting.

Ear Cleaning

Cleaning your puppy's ears is an essential part of their grooming routine. It helps to prevent ear infections and other ear-related health issues.

Step 1: Use a cotton ball or soft cloth to wipe the inside of your puppy's ears. Make sure that you avoid using cotton swabs, as these can push the wax and debris further into their ears.

Step 2: Apply a few drops of a specially formulated ear cleaning solution to their ears. This can help to loosen and remove any remaining wax or debris.

Step 3: Gently massage the base of your puppy's ears for a few minutes. This will help to distribute the ear cleaning solution and loosen any remaining debris.

Step 4: Use a cotton ball or soft cloth to wipe away any remaining debris or excess ear cleaning solution.

Remember to always use gentle strokes and be patient with your puppy during the grooming process. With a little love and attention, you can help your furry friend to look and feel their best.

Trim Nails

Overgrown nails can cause discomfort, pain and even lead to injury. Trim your pet's nails regularly, taking care not to cut the quick (the blood vessel that runs through the nail).

Health Care

Regular check-ups at the veterinarian are important for your pet's health. Here are some ways to keep your pet healthy:

Schedule Regular Check-Ups: Schedule regular check-ups with your veterinarian to ensure your pet is healthy and up-to-date on vaccinations.

Address Health Issues Promptly: If your pet displays signs of illness or injury, contact your veterinarian promptly.

Follow Preventative Care Measures: Preventative care measures, such as regular flea and tick treatments and heartworm prevention, can help keep your pet healthy and prevent the spread of disease.

In conclusion, providing your pet with basic care and maintenance, including feeding and watering, grooming, and health care, is essential for their health and happiness. By choosing a high-quality diet, grooming your pet regularly, and scheduling regular check-ups with your veterinarian, you can help ensure your pet stays healthy and happy for years to come.

II

The ABCs of Dog Training: Basic Commands for a Well-Behaved Pup

5

Creating a Positive Learning Environment

When it comes to training a puppy, creating a positive learning environment is key. This environment should be safe and comfortable for your puppy, and it should foster a positive relationship between you and your furry friend. In this chapter, we will discuss how to set up a safe and comfortable space, create a positive relationship with your puppy, and choose the right training tools.

Setting up a Safe and Comfortable Space

Before you begin training your puppy, it's important to set up a safe and comfortable space for them. This space should be free from any potential hazards or distractions, such as loose cords, sharp objects, or loud noises.

When it comes to training your puppy, choosing the right training tools can make all the difference. Some of the most popular training tools include clickers, treat pouches, and training collars.

Clickers are a great way to signal to your puppy that they have done something right, while treat pouches make it easy to reward good behavior on the go.

Training collars, such as prong collars or choke chains, should be used with caution and only under the guidance of a professional trainer.

In addition, there are also a variety of training aids available, such as crates, potty pads, and training pads. Crates can be a great way to provide your puppy with a comfortable and safe space to relax and sleep, while potty pads and training pads can help to encourage good potty training habits. In the next chapters, we will discuss these trainings in-depth, and you will discover step-by-step instructions for each one of them.

CREATING A POSITIVE LEARNING ENVIRONMENT

Here are ten tips that have been proven to improve dog training effectiveness by professional trainers:

- Use positive reinforcement exercises to reward good behavior and ignore bad behavior.
- Keep training sessions short and frequent, rather than long and infrequent.
- Be consistent with your commands and training techniques.
- Start with basic and easy commands, such as sit, stay, and come, before proceeding to more advanced training.
- Train in a quiet, distraction-free environment to help your dog focus on the training.
- Gradually increase the level of difficulty in the training as your dog becomes more proficient.
- Use treats and toys as motivators to encourage your dog to learn.
- Use a variety of training techniques, including clicker training and shaping, to keep training interesting for your dog.
- Avoid punishment-based training methods, as they can be counterproductive and damaging to your dog's trust in you.
- Be consistent and patient in the process, as it may take time for your dog to learn new behaviors and commands.

Creating a positive learning environment is essential when it comes to training your puppy. By setting up a safe and comfortable space, creating a positive relationship with your puppy, and choosing the right training tools, you can help to ensure that your furry friend enjoys the training process and is successful in learning new behaviors.

6

Development Stages

Bringing a new puppy home can be thrilling, but it also comes with responsibilities. One of the most crucial aspects of puppy ownership is training. Training your puppy is an essential part of owning a dog. It helps establish good behavior and socialization skills that will last throughout their lives. However, training should be done in a manner that is age-appropriate for your puppy's developmental stage.

The Neonatal Stage (Week 1 - 2)

During this stage, puppies are blind and deaf, and they rely solely on their mother for survival. At this point, the attention should be on providing a safe, warm, and clean environment for the puppies to thrive. There is no need for formal training at this stage, but gentle handling can help the puppies get used to human touch.

The Transition Stage (Week 3 - 4)

During the transition stage, the puppies' eyes and ears begin to open, and they become more aware of their surroundings. This is a crucial period for socialization, and it's important to expose the puppies to different sights, sounds, and smells. Puppies should also begin to learn basic behaviors such as responding to their name, coming when called, and basic potty training.

The Socialization Stage (Week 5 - 7)

During this stage, puppies become more adventurous and playful. They are more aware of their littermates and begin to learn important social skills such as bite inhibition and play behavior. This is also the ideal time for crate training and more advanced potty training techniques.

The Juvenile Stage (Week 8 - 16)

During the juvenile stage, puppies become more independent and start to test their boundaries. This is the ideal time to start more formal training such as sit, stay, and heel. It's important to keep training sessions short and fun to keep your puppy engaged.

The Adolescent Stage (Week 16 - 52)

During this stage, puppies enter adolescence and can become more stubborn and independent. This is a challenging time for dog owners, and it's important to continue training and socialization to prevent any behavior issues from developing. Advanced training such as recall and off-leash training can be introduced at this stage.

Training your puppy is a crucial part of responsible dog ownership. By understanding your puppy's developmental stages, you can provide appropriate training and socialization that will help them develop into well-behaved and confident adult dogs. Remember to keep training fun and engaging, and always use positive reinforcement techniques to ensure a positive training experience for both you and your puppy.

7

Training Older Dogs

Training older dogs can be a bit more challenging than training puppies, but it's still possible to teach an old dog new tricks. Older dogs have established behaviors, and they may have developed bad habits that need to be addressed. In this chapter, we will explore the differences between training older dogs and puppies, what type of training is important for older dogs, and how to do it effectively.

Understanding the differences between training older dogs and puppies

Older dogs have already developed their personalities and habits, which makes them different from puppies. They have had more life experiences, and some may have even been through traumatic events. As a result, older dogs may require a different approach to training than puppies.

Additionally, older dogs may have physical limitations that can affect their ability to learn new behaviors. They may also have medical conditions that require special care or attention during training. It's important to keep these factors in mind when training older dogs.

What type of training is important for older dogs?

Training older dogs can focus on correcting bad behaviors or teaching new behaviors. However, it's important to start with basic obedience commands, such as sit, stay, come, and down. These commands can help establish a foundation for more advanced training.

In addition, training older dogs can focus on improving their physical and mental health. For example, teaching them to walk on a leash or providing puzzle toys can help keep their minds and bodies active.

How to do it effectively

When training older dogs, it's important to keep training sessions short and positive. Older dogs may not have the same energy or stamina as younger dogs, so it's important to avoid overwhelming them with long training sessions.

Positive reinforcement techniques, such as treats and praise, are essential for training older dogs. This approach can help build trust and strengthen the bond between the dog and owner.

It's also important to be patient and understanding when training older dogs. They may take longer to learn new behaviors, but with consistency and patience, they can still make progress.

Bringing home a new dog when you already have a furry friend

If you bring home a new dog who is older, it's important to approach training with sensitivity and understanding. Here are some tips to keep in mind:

Give both dogs space and time to adjust

It's important to give both dogs time and space to get used to each other. This may involve keeping them separated at first and gradually introducing them under supervision.

Address any behavior issues

If your older dog has any behavior issues, such as aggression or anxiety, it's important to address these before introducing a new dog. Seek the help of a professional trainer or behaviorist if necessary.

Be patient and understanding

Both dogs will need time to adjust to each other and establish their place in the household. Be patient and understanding, and don't force them to interact if they are not ready.

Provide separate resources

It's important to provide separate resources, such as food bowls and toys, to prevent any territorial behavior. This can also help prevent conflicts between the dogs.

Training should be done separately

When training both dogs, it's important to do it separately. This will help prevent competition between the dogs and ensure that each dog gets the attention and training they need.

Introducing a new dog into a household with an older dog requires patience and understanding. Addressing any behavior issues and providing separate resources are important to prevent conflicts. Training should be done separately, and consistency is key to successful training. With time and patience, both dogs can learn to coexist and form a bond with each other.

In conclusion, training older dogs requires a different approach than training puppies. Older dogs have established behaviors and may have physical limitations that need to be taken into account. Basic obedience commands, improving their physical and mental health, and positive reinforcement techniques are important for training older dogs. With patience and consistency, it's possible to teach an old dog new tricks and strengthen the bond between the dog and owner.

8

Crate Training

Crate training is a popular and effective method for house training a new puppy. A crate is a small, enclosed space that provides a safe and comfortable environment for your puppy to rest and relax in. Crate training can be beneficial for both the puppy and the owner, as it helps to prevent destructive behavior, separation anxiety, and other issues.

Why Crate Training is Important

Using a crate is important for several reasons. Firstly, it helps to prevent accidents and damage to your home. Puppies are naturally curious and like to explore their surroundings, but they can also be destructive if left alone. By providing your puppy with a crate, you can keep them safe and secure while you are away.

Secondly, crate training can help with house training. Dogs are naturally clean animals and will avoid soiling their sleeping area. By keeping your puppy in a crate, you can teach them to hold their bladder and bowels until you take them outside. This can be especially useful during the night or when you are unable to supervise your puppy.

Finally, crate training can help to prevent separation anxiety. Dogs are social animals and thrive on human interaction. However, they also need time to rest and relax on their own. By providing your puppy with a crate, you can teach them to feel comfortable and secure when they are alone, which can help to prevent anxiety and other behavioral problems.

Size, Type, and Material of Crate

When choosing a crate for your puppy, there are several factors to consider, including size, type, and material.

Size

Size is an important consideration when selecting a crate. The crate should be large enough for your puppy to stand up, turn around, and lie down comfortably. However, it should not be so large that your puppy has room to roam around or use one end as a bathroom. A good rule of thumb is to select a crate that is one and a half times the length of your puppy from nose to tail.

Material

Material is also an important consideration when selecting a crate. The crate should be made of a sturdy and durable material that can withstand the wear and tear of daily use. It should also be easy to clean and maintain, as puppies can be messy and prone to accidents.

Plastic crates

Plastic crates are durable, secure, and easy to clean. The enclosed design creates a cozy den-like space for the puppy, which can help with anxiety and crate training. Some models are also airline-approved, making it easier to travel with your puppy.

Wire crates

Wire crates provide good visibility and air circulation, and usually have removable trays for easy cleaning. They are also versatile and can be used for crate training or as a playpen. However, puppies who are still learning to control their bladder may have accidents in the crate which can be difficult to clean from the wire mesh.

Soft-sided crates

Not recommended for puppies as they are less durable and can be chewed or clawed through. They are also not suitable for puppies who are not yet crate trained as the soft sides do not provide the same enclosed den-like space that a plastic or wire crate does.

Wooden crates

Wooden crates are not as durable and can be chewed or scratched easily. Additionally, they may not provide enough ventilation for the puppy and can be difficult to clean.

Fabric crates

Fabric crates are not as durable as other types of crates and can be easily destroyed by chewing or clawing. They are also not recommended for puppies who are not yet crate trained as the fabric may not provide enough security and can be easily torn.

Let's get started with the training!

Before you start training your puppy, you need to make sure you have the right crate. It should be big enough for your puppy to stand up, turn around, and lie down in comfortably, but not so big that they can use one end as a bathroom and the other as a sleeping area. The crate should also be sturdy and secure, with a door that latches properly.

1. Introduce the Crate

Once you have the crate, start by introducing it to your puppy. Let them explore the crate on their own and get comfortable with it. You can do this by placing treats or toys inside the crate and letting your puppy go in and out at their own pace.

2. Feed Your Puppy in the Crate

One way to get your puppy used to the crate is to feed them their meals inside it. This will help them associate the crate with positive experiences and create a positive association with being inside.

3. Use Positive Reinforcement

Whenever your puppy goes inside the crate voluntarily, praise and reward them with treats or toys. This will help reinforce the behavior and encourage them to continue using the crate.

4. Gradually Increase Time in the Crate

Once your puppy is comfortable going in and out of the crate, start increasing the amount of time they spend inside. Begin by closing the door for just a few seconds, then gradually work up to longer periods of time.

5. Don't Leave Your Puppy Alone for Too Long

When you first start crate training, it's important not to leave your puppy alone for too long. They may become anxious or upset if they are left alone in the crate for extended periods of time. Gradually increase the length of time you leave them in the crate, starting with just a few minutes and working up to longer periods of time.

6. Keep the Crate Clean

Make sure to keep the crate clean and free of any messes or accidents. This will help your puppy associate the crate with a clean and comfortable space.

7. Be Patient

Remember, crate training takes time and patience. It may take several weeks or even months for your puppy to become fully comfortable with the crate. Be patient and consistent in your training, and your puppy will eventually learn to love their crate as a safe and comfortable space.

In conclusion, crate training is a valuable tool for house training your new puppy. By selecting the right size, type, and material of crate, you can provide your puppy with a safe and comfortable environment that will help to prevent accidents, promote good behavior, and reduce anxiety. With patience, consistency, and positive reinforcement, crate training can be an effective way to teach your puppy to be a well-behaved and happy member of your family.

9

Potty Training

Potty training is one of the most essential aspects of training a new puppy. It can be challenging, but it is a crucial step in raising a happy and healthy pet. In this chapter, we will discuss the importance of potty training for puppies and pet owners.

Potty training is a critical aspect of puppy training that helps establish good hygiene practices and develops a clean living environment for your pet. Training your puppy to go potty in the right place ensures that your home remains clean and hygienic, reducing the chances of unpleasant smells and bacterial growth that can cause infections.

Potty training not only benefits the puppy but also helps the pet owner in many ways. A potty trained puppy reduces the amount of time spent cleaning up messes and accidents, reduces the chances of damage to furniture, and saves money by reducing the need for cleaning supplies and replacement of damaged items.

Understanding Your Puppy's Potty Needs

Before beginning to train your puppy, it is important to understand their potty needs. Puppies have smaller bladders and require more frequent potty breaks compared to adult dogs.

Puppies need to go potty frequently because their digestive systems are still developing. They process food quickly and produce waste more frequently than adult dogs.

It is essential to learn how to recognize the signs that your puppy needs to go potty.

Common signs include:

- Sniffing
- Restlessness
- Circling
- Whining

What you need to know before the training

Establishing a routine is critical when potty training your puppy. Consistency and predictability are essential for successful training. To establish a routine, you should feed your puppy at the same time every day and take them out for potty breaks at regular intervals. It is best to take your puppy out after meals, naps, and playtime.

1.Choosing a Potty Spot

Choosing a designated potty spot is crucial for effective potty training. A consistent spot will help your puppy learn where to go and what is expected of them. The ideal potty spot for your puppy should be outside and away from their living area. Avoid areas with high foot traffic or where other dogs frequently go potty. Having a designated potty area helps to prevent accidents and makes cleanup easier. Your puppy will also learn that this is where they should go potty.

2. Training Your Puppy to Use the Designated Spot

Training your puppy to use the designated spot involves consistently taking them to the same spot, using verbal commands, and rewarding good behavior.

3. Dealing with Accidents

Accidents will happen during the potty training process. However, it is essential to handle them properly to prevent setbacks in the training process.

4. How to Clean Up Accidents Properly

Clean up accidents properly by using an enzymatic cleaner to remove the scent completely. Avoid using ammonia-based cleaners as they may attract your puppy to the same spot.

5. Preventing Accidents from Happening in the Future

To prevent accidents from happening in the future, make sure to supervise your puppy and take them out for potty breaks regularly. You can also limit their access to certain areas of the house until they are fully potty trained.

5. What Not to Do When Your Puppy Has an Accident

Do not punish your puppy for accidents, as this can create fear and anxiety. Instead, redirect their behavior to the designated potty spot and use positive reinforcement to encourage good behavior.

Common Potty Training Challenges and Solutions

Potty training can present some challenges, but with patience and consistency, you can overcome them:

Common Challenges

- Accidents inside the house
- Not signaling or communicating their need to go outside
- Difficulty understanding the designated potty area
- Fear or reluctance to go outside
- Distractions and lack of focus during potty breaks
- Going potty too frequently or not frequently enough
- Regression or setbacks in previously learned potty training habits

Solutions

- Establish a consistent routine for potty breaks and stick to it
- Use positive reinforcement, such as treats or praise, when your puppy goes potty outside
- Supervise your puppy closely and limit their access to areas where accidents may occur
- Use a designated potty area and take your puppy to that spot every time they need to go
- Create a positive association with going outside by playing or giving attention after potty breaks
- Consider crate training or confining your puppy to a small space when you can't be around them
- Be patient and consistent in your training, and don't punish your puppy for accidents or mistakes.

Note: Puppies may experience anxiety or fear during the potty training process. You can help them feel more comfortable by providing a safe and secure environment, using positive reinforcement, and avoiding punishment.

Addressing Marking Behaviors

Marking behaviors involve urinating to mark territory or assert dominance. To address this behavior, it is essential to provide enough physical and mental stimulation and avoid punishment.

Here are some ways to provide physical and mental stimulation:

Physical Stimulation:

- Play fetch with a ball or a toy.
- Take your puppy for walks or runs.
- Let your puppy play with other dogs.
- Play tug-of-war with a rope toy.
- Create an obstacle course for your puppy to navigate.
- Go for a hike with your puppy.
- Teach your puppy to swim.
- Use a flirt pole to play with your puppy.
- Play hide-and-seek with your puppy.
- Set up a puppy playdate.

Mental Stimulation:

- Teach your puppy new tricks.
- Use puzzle toys to challenge your puppy's mind.
- Play "find the treat" with your puppy.
- Use scent work activities to challenge your puppy's nose.
- Train your puppy in obedience and agility.
- Let your puppy play with different textures and surfaces.
- Rotate your puppy's toys to keep them engaged.

- Use clicker training to teach your puppy new skills.
- Teach your puppy to use their sense of hearing and touch.
- Play games that require problem-solving skills, such as "hide the toy."

Puppies may resist potty training for various reasons, such as a lack of consistency, improper training, or health issues. To overcome resistance, make sure to be consistent with your training and use positive reinforcement.

Potty training is an essential aspect of puppy training that helps establish good hygiene practices and a clean living environment for your pet. Understanding your puppy's potty needs, establishing a routine, choosing a designated potty spot, and using positive reinforcement are critical for successful potty training. With patience and consistency, you can overcome common challenges and enjoy the benefits of a potty-trained puppy.

10

Basic Commands

Training a puppy can be a fun and rewarding experience for both the puppy and the owner, but it requires patience, consistency, and understanding of the fundamentals of puppy training. In this chapter, we will discuss the basic principles of puppy training and what every puppy owner should know before they start training.

First and foremost, it's important to understand that puppies have a short attention span and limited ability to focus. They also have a natural tendency to chew, bite, and play rough, which can make training challenging. Therefore, it's crucial to start training as early as possible to establish good habits and prevent unwanted behaviors from becoming ingrained.

Teaching Basic Commands

Teaching your puppy basic commands is an essential part of their training. These commands will not only make your life easier but also help to keep your furry friend safe and well-behaved. In this chapter, we will dive even deeper into the basics. We will teach your puppy to sit, stay, and come, as well as how to teach them to walk on a leash and wait.

Teaching Your Puppy to Sit

Teaching your puppy to sit is one of the most basic and important commands.

1.To do this, start by holding a treat close to your puppy's nose and then move it slowly up and back towards their ears.

2.As your puppy follows the treat with their head, their bottom should naturally lower to the ground.

3.Once your puppy is in a sitting position, say "sit" and give them the treat. 4.Repeat this process several times a day until your puppy associates the command with the behavior.

Teaching Your Puppy to Stay

1.Start by having your puppy sit.

2.Then, hold your hand up in front of them with your palm facing out and say "stay".

3.Step back a few feet and wait for a few seconds before returning to your puppy and giving them a treat.

4.Gradually increase the amount of time you ask your puppy to stay before giving them a treat.

5.If your puppy gets up before you release them, say "no" and start again.

Teaching Your Puppy to Come

Teaching your puppy to come is crucial for their safety.

1.To do this, start by having your puppy on a leash and then take a few steps away from them.

2.Say "come" in a friendly tone of voice and then gently pull the leash towards you.

3.When your puppy reaches you, give them a treat and praise them.

4.Incrementally increase the distance between you and your puppy and decrease the amount of leash pulling as your puppy becomes more proficient.

Training Your Puppy to Walk on a Leash

Walking on a leash is an incredibly useful skill for both you and your furry friend.

1.To do this, start by attaching the leash to your puppy's collar and then let them get used to the weight of it.

2.Once they are comfortable, start walking with them and give them a treat and praise when they walk nicely by your side.

3.If your puppy pulls on the leash, stand still and wait for them to come back to your side before continuing.

4.Incrementally increase the amount of time and distance you walk with your puppy on a leash.

Teaching Your Puppy to Wait

Teaching your puppy to wait is a useful command for a variety of situations, such as waiting for food or waiting to be released from a crate.

1. Start by having your puppy sit and then hold your hand up in front of them with your palm facing out.

2. Say "wait" and take a step back.

3. If your puppy stays in the sitting position, give them a treat and praise them.

4. Make sure you increase the amount of time and distance you ask your puppy to wait.

Teaching your puppy basic commands is an essential part of their training. By teaching them to sit, stay, and come, as well as walk on a leash and wait, you can help to keep your furry friend safe and well-behaved. Remember to use positive reinforcement tools, such as treats and praise, and to be patient and consistent in your training. With practice and time, your puppy will become proficient in these basic commands and be ready to move on to more advanced training.

III

Beyond Sit and Stay: Advanced Training and Health Tips for a Happy Dog

11

Advanced Training

Advanced training is crucial for developing a well-rounded and obedient puppy. Training is not only about building skills, but it also helps establish an unbreakable bond between the puppy and the owner. It teaches the puppy to respect and trust the owner while improving their overall behavior. An advanced training program helps to curb undesirable behaviors such as jumping, biting, and barking, and helps to promote good behaviors such as responding to commands, staying calm in stressful situations, and remaining obedient in public.

The benefits of advanced training for puppies are vast, and they include:

Improved Behavior: Advanced training helps to improve a puppy's behavior and obedience. It teaches the puppy to be respectful, patient, and obedient around people and other dogs.

Increased Socialization: Advanced training provides an opportunity for puppies to interact with other people, dogs, and environments, which helps to build confidence, reduce anxiety, and promote socialization.

Better Communication: Advanced training helps to improve communication between the puppy and the owner. It teaches the owner to understand their puppy's body language and respond appropriately to their needs.

Increased Mental and Physical Stimulation: Advanced training provides puppies with the necessary mental and physical stimulation to keep them engaged, challenged, and stimulated. It helps to promote healthy development and growth.

Bonding: Advanced training helps to build a strong bond between the puppy and the owner. The training process helps to establish trust and respect, which promotes a happy and healthy relationship between the puppy and the owner.

Advanced Training Techniques

Clicker Training

1. Introduce the clicker to your puppy and associate the sound of the clicker with a treat. For example, click the clicker and immediately give your puppy a treat. Repeat this process several times until the puppy understands the association between the clicker and a treat.
2. Begin training with a more complex command, such as "roll over." Say the command and wait for the puppy to respond. When the puppy rolls over, click the clicker and give a treat.
3. Repeat the process, gradually increasing the difficulty of the commands. You can try different variations of the command, such as "roll over to the right" or "roll over to the left." Remember to click the clicker immediately after the puppy performs the desired behavior and reward with a treat.
4. As your puppy becomes more advanced, you can start using the clicker to shape behavior for more complex tricks, such as "play dead" or "crawl."

Positive Reinforcement Training

1. Choose a more complex command, such as "shake hands." Say the command and wait for the puppy to respond. When the puppy shakes hands, immediately reward with a treat, praise, or toy.
2. Repeat the process, gradually increasing the difficulty of the commands. You can try different variations of the command, such as "high five" or "gimme five." Remember to reward the puppy immediately after the desired behavior.
3. Avoid punishing or scolding the puppy for undesirable behavior. Instead, ignore the behavior and reward the puppy for desirable behavior.
4. As your puppy becomes more advanced, you can start using positive reinforcement to shape behavior for more complex tricks, such as "wave goodbye" or "spin around."

Conditioning Training

1. Choose a more complex command, such as "jump through the hoop." Every time you ring the bell or blow the whistle, immediately give your puppy a treat.
2. Repeat the process several times until the puppy associates the sound of the bell or whistle with a treat. Then, start training by saying the command and ringing the bell or blowing the whistle. When the puppy jumps through the hoop, immediately give a treat.
3. Repeat the process, gradually increasing the difficulty of the

commands. You can try different variations of the command, such as "jump through the hoop backwards" or "jump through the hoop twice." Remember to ring the bell or blow the whistle immediately before the puppy performs the desired behavior and reward with a treat.
4. As your puppy becomes more advanced, you can start using conditioning training to shape behavior for more complex tricks, such as "jump through a ring of fire" or "jump over a hurdle."

As puppies grow and learn, it is important to teach them advanced commands that will improve their behavior, increase their mental stimulation, and provide them with a sense of accomplishment. Continue reading to find step-by-step instructions for the above mentioned commands.

Off-leash Training

Off-leash training is an essential skill for puppies as it allows them to explore their environment while remaining safe and under control. Before starting off-leash training, make sure that your puppy has mastered basic obedience commands such as "sit," "stay," and "come" while on a leash.

Step 1: Find a secure and enclosed area where your puppy can run freely without getting lost or hurt.

Step 2: Attach a long lead to your puppy's collar and let them explore the area while holding onto the lead.

Step 3: As your puppy explores, call their name and give the command "come." When your puppy comes to you, reward them with a treat or praise.

Step 4: Gradually increase the distance between you and your puppy, and practice calling them back to you using the "come" command.

Step 5: Once your puppy is consistently coming back to you, you can remove the lead and practice off-leash training in a safe and enclosed area.

Advanced Obedience Commands

Heel

Step 1: Attach a leash to your puppy's collar and stand to their left side.

Step 2: Give the command "heel" and start walking.

Step 3: If your puppy starts to pull, stop and give the command "sit." Once your puppy is sitting, start again.

Step 4: Gradually increase the distance and duration of the heel command.

Tricks

Tricks such as "play dead," "roll over," and "speak" are fun and entertaining for both puppies and their owners.

Roll over

Step 1: Start by commanding your puppy to "lie down."

Step 2: Hold a treat in front of your puppy's nose and slowly move it towards their shoulder.

Step 3: As your puppy follows the treat, their body will naturally roll over.

Step 4: Once your puppy has rolled over, reward them with the treat or praise.

Play dead

Step 1: Start by commanding your puppy to "lie down."

Step 2: Hold a treat in front of your puppy's nose and slowly move it towards the ground.

Step 3: As your puppy follows the treat, gently lay them on their side and say "play dead."

Step 4: Reward your puppy with a treat or praise.

Speak

Step 1: Hold a treat in front of your puppy's nose and wait for them to bark.

Step 2: As soon as your puppy barks, give the command "speak" and reward them with the treat or praise.

Step 3: Practice this command several times until your puppy starts to associate the command with the act of barking.

Step 4: Once your puppy has mastered the "speak" command, you can start working on the "quiet" command by saying "quiet" and rewarding your puppy when they stop barking.

In conclusion, teaching your puppy advanced commands such as off-leash training, advanced obedience commands, and tricks will not only improve their behavior and provide them with mental stimulation, but it will also strengthen the bond between your furry friend and you. Remember to be patient, consistent, and positive during the training process, and most importantly, have fun with your puppy!

12

Socialization Training

Socialization is a crucial aspect in the development of a puppy, as it helps them to build confidence, reduce anxiety, and learn appropriate behavior around people and other dogs. In this chapter, we will cover some of the most important aspects of socialization training and provide step-by-step instructions for introducing puppies to new people, animals, and environments.

Introducing Puppies to Animals, New People, and Environments

One of the most important aspects of socialization is introducing puppies to new people, animals, and environments. This will help them to become comfortable and confident in different situations and avoid developing fear or aggression towards unfamiliar stimuli.

Step 1: Start by exposing your puppy to different types of people, animals, and environments at a young age. This will help them to become accustomed to new experiences and reduce the likelihood of fear or anxiety.

Step 2: Always supervise your puppy when introducing them to new people, animals, or environments. This will ensure that they are safe and that their interactions are positive.

Step 3: Use treats or positive reinforcement to encourage your puppy. This will help them to associate these experiences with positive outcomes.

Step 4: If your puppy displays inappropriate behavior such as growling or nipping, redirect their attention to a toy or treat and remove them from the situation.

Building Confidence and Reducing Anxiety

Socialization can also help to build confidence and reduce anxiety in puppies.

Step 1: Start by exposing your puppy to new experiences in a controlled and positive environment. This could include new toys, new sounds, or new environments.

Step 2: If your puppy displays signs of anxiety or fear such as shaking or panting, redirect their attention to a treat or a toy and remove them from the situation.

Socialization is an important aspect of a puppy's development as it helps them to build confidence, reduce anxiety, and learn appropriate behavior around people and other dogs. Remember to always supervise your puppy during socialization and use positive reinforcement to encourage appropriate behavior. With consistency and patience, you can help your puppy to become a well-socialized and confident adult dog.

13

Agility Training

Agility training is a fun and rewarding activity for both puppies and their owners. It involves running through an obstacle course that includes jumps, tunnels, weave poles, and other obstacles. Agility training can help to develop coordination, agility, and overall fitness in puppies. In this chapter, we will cover the introduction to agility obstacles and provide step-by-step instructions for developing coordination and agility in puppies.

Introduction to Agility Obstacles

The first step in agility training is introducing puppies to the different obstacles they will encounter on the course.

Step 1: Start with simple obstacles such as a low jump or a tunnel that is open at both ends. This will help your puppy to become familiar with the concept of agility obstacles.

Step 2: Use treats or positive reinforcement to encourage your puppy to approach and go through the obstacles. This will help them to associate the obstacles with positive outcomes.

Step 3: Gradually increase the difficulty of the obstacles over time. This could include increasing the height of the jumps or adding more complex obstacles such as weave poles.

Step 4: Always supervise your puppy during agility training to ensure their safety and to provide positive reinforcement for appropriate behavior.

Developing Coordination and Agility in Puppies

Step 1: Start with basic exercises such as running in circles or playing fetch. This will help your puppy to develop coordination and agility.

Step 2: Use positive reinforcement to encourage your puppy to engage in these exercises. This could include treats, toys, or praise.

Step 3: Incorporate agility obstacles into your puppy's exercise routine. This will help them to develop coordination and agility in a fun and engaging way.

Remember to always supervise your puppy during agility training and to use positive reinforcement to encourage appropriate behavior. With patience and consistency, you can help your puppy to become a skilled and confident agility dog.

In this guide, we have covered the importance and benefits of advanced training for puppies. We discussed the different types of advanced training, including off-leash training, advanced obedience commands, socialization training, and agility training. Each type of training is designed to help puppies develop important skills and behaviors that will serve them well throughout their lives.

Advanced training for puppies offers a wide range of benefits. It can help to develop their physical and mental abilities, increase their confidence and socialization skills, and strengthen the bond between them and their owners. With advanced training, puppies can learn to navigate the world around them with ease, adapt to new situations, and become well-behaved and obedient pets.

As a puppy owner, it is important to pursue advanced training for your pet. Not only will it benefit them, but it will also provide you with the satisfaction of watching your puppy grow and learn new skills. Whether you choose to pursue advanced training through a professional trainer or on your own, the key is to remain patient and consistent with your puppy.

14

Behavior Modification

Behavior modification training involves addressing and managing problem behaviors in dogs. This chapter will discuss common problem behaviors: excessive barking, biting, and aggression, as well as separation anxiety. We will also cover the techniques of counter-conditioning and desensitization, which are effective methods for modifying unwanted behaviors.

Understanding and Managing Problem Behaviors

Excessive Barking

Excessive barking can be a nuisance to both dogs and their owners. Some common causes of excessive barking include fear, boredom, anxiety, territorial behavior, and attention-seeking. To manage excessive barking, it's important to identify the root cause of the behavior and address it.

- Identify the cause of the excessive barking.
- Redirect your dog's attention to a more appropriate behavior, such as sitting or lying down, and reward them for this behavior.
- Teach your dog the "quiet" command by saying the word "quiet" when they bark and rewarding them when they stop barking.
- Use positive reinforcement to reinforce quiet behavior and redirect attention when necessary.

Biting and Aggression

Biting and aggression can be dangerous behaviors and require careful management and training. Common causes of biting and aggression include fear, territorial behavior, and lack of socialization. It's important to consult with a professional dog trainer or behaviorist for guidance in managing and modifying these behaviors.

- Consult with a behaviorist or professional dog trainer to assess the severity and cause of the biting or aggression behavior.
- Follow the trainer or behaviorist's recommended training techniques and management strategies.
- Use positive reinforcement to reinforce calm and non-aggressive behavior.
- Avoid punishing or physically correcting your dog, as this can exacerbate aggressive behavior.

Addressing Separation Anxiety

Separation anxiety is a common problem behavior in dogs and can cause destructive behavior and distress. Signs of separation anxiety include excessive barking, destructive chewing, and house soiling. To address separation anxiety, it's important to gradually acclimate your dog to being alone and to make their alone time more comfortable and enjoyable.

- Gradually acclimate your dog to being alone by leaving them alone for short periods of time and gradually increasing the length of time.
- Provide your dog with comfort items, such as a favorite toy or blanket, to make their alone time more enjoyable.
- Create a safe and comfortable space for your dog, such as a crate or a designated room.
- Use positive reinforcement to reward calm and non-destructive behavior when you return home.

Counter-Conditioning and Desensitization

Counter-conditioning and desensitization are effective techniques for modifying unwanted behaviors by gradually exposing the dog to the stimulus that triggers the behavior in a controlled and positive environment.

- Identify the stimulus that triggers the unwanted behavior.
- Gradually expose your dog to the stimulus in a controlled and positive environment.
- Reward calm and non-reactive behavior in response to the stimulus.
- Gradually increase the intensity or duration of the exposure as your dog becomes more comfortable with the stimulus.

Negative Reinforcement Techniques

Negative reinforcement is another technique for correcting bad behaviors in dogs. This technique involves removing or withholding something unpleasant when the dog exhibits good behavior. For example, if a dog jumps on guests, the owner can turn away from the dog and withhold attention until the dog calms down. This technique can be particularly effective for behaviors that are attention-seeking, such as jumping or barking.

Another negative reinforcement technique is time outs. Time outs involve removing the dog from a situation or area when the dog exhibits bad behavior. For example, if a dog is barking excessively, the owner can put the dog in a separate room until the barking stops. This technique can be particularly effective for behaviors that are disruptive or dangerous, such as aggressive behavior.

The Use of Punishment

Punishment is a controversial technique for correcting bad behaviors in dogs. Punishment involves the use of something unpleasant, such as a shock collar or yelling, to discourage bad behavior. While punishment can be effective in stopping a behavior in the short term, it can be harmful to the dog and may cause long-term behavior problems.

Studies have shown that punishment can lead to fear, anxiety, and aggression in dogs. In addition, punishment can damage the relationship between the owner and the dog, as the dog may associate the punishment with the owner.

Positive and negative reinforcement techniques are often more effective and humane than punishment. These techniques focus on rewarding good behavior and withholding rewards for bad behavior. Over time, the dog learns that good behavior is rewarded, and will be more likely to repeat that behavior in the future.

Behavior modification training requires patience, consistency, and a deep understanding of your dog's behavior and communication. By using positive reinforcement and gradual exposure techniques, you can effectively modify problem behaviors and improve your dog's quality of life. Remember to always consult with a professional dog trainer or behaviorist for guidance and support in managing and modifying your dog's behavior.

IV

Mental Exercises For A Sharp Dog

15

Mental Exercise

Just like humans, dogs need regular exercise to stay healthy and happy. However, physical exercise is not the only type of activity that is important for your furry friend. Mental exercise is just as crucial to keep your dog's mind sharp and prevent boredom and destructive behavior. In this chapter, we'll explore what mental exercise is and give you ten examples to try with your dog.

What is Mental Exercise?

Mental exercise involves engaging your dog's mind in various ways to challenge and stimulate their cognitive abilities. These types of exercises help improve your dog's problem-solving skills, increase their focus and concentration, and provide a sense of mental satisfaction that is equally important as physical exercise.

Here are examples of mental exercises you can try with your dog:

Puzzle toys

Puzzle toys are an excellent way to provide mental stimulation for dogs. They come in various shapes and sizes, but all have one thing in common: they challenge your dog's cognitive abilities by requiring them to solve a puzzle to access their food or treats. Here are some examples of puzzle toys and how they stimulate dogs:

Kong Classic: This classic puzzle toy is made of durable rubber and can be filled with treats or peanut butter. The unique shape and texture of the toy encourage dogs to chew and lick, providing mental and physical stimulation.

Outward Hound Nina Ottosson Dog Tornado Puzzle Toy: This toy requires dogs to rotate the layers of the toy to access hidden treats. It helps dogs develop problem-solving skills and improves their focus and concentration.

Trixie Pet Products Flip Board: This puzzle toy has different compartments that require dogs to use their paws and nose to flip open and access hidden treats. It helps improve a dog's problem-solving skills and mental agility.

PetSafe Busy Buddy Twist 'n Treat: This puzzle toy is designed to be filled with treats and adjusted to different difficulty levels. It challenges dogs to figure out how to twist the toy to release the treats, providing mental and physical stimulation.

Kyjen Hide-A-Squirrel Puzzle Toy: This puzzle toy comes with a stuffed tree trunk and several squeaky squirrels that dogs have to remove from the trunk. It encourages dogs to use their nose and paws to retrieve the squirrels, providing mental and physical stimulation.

Hide-and-Seek

Hide and seek can provide mental exercise for your dog. It engages their mind and requires them to use their senses to navigate and explore their environment. Hide and seek can also be a fun way to reinforce training. For example, you can hide a favorite toy and encourage your dog to find it using a specific command, such as "find it." This reinforces their training and strengthens their bond with you.

Learning new tricks

Teaching your dog new tricks is not only fun but can also provide a great mental workout. Tricks that require your dog to think and problem-solve can be especially stimulating for your furry friend.

Shake hands/paws: Teaching your dog to shake hands or paws can be a fun trick that provides mental stimulation. It requires your dog to focus on your hand and understand the command, which engages their cognitive abilities.

Play dead: Teaching your dog to play dead is a more challenging trick that requires them to understand complex commands and learn a new behavior. It stimulates their problem-solving skills and encourages them to think outside the box.

Spin: Teaching your dog to spin is a fun and engaging trick that requires them to understand the command and follow a specific motion. It helps improve your dog's coordination and balance, as well as their mental focus and agility.

High five: Teaching your dog to give a high five is a cute and interactive trick that requires them to understand the command and use their paws in a specific way. It helps improve their coordination and mental focus.

Roll over: Teaching your dog to roll over is a more complex trick that requires them to learn a new behavior and understand complex commands. It helps stimulate their problem-solving skills and encourages them to think in different ways.

Agility training

Set up an obstacle course with jumps, tunnels, and weaving poles.

Scent work: Train your dog to identify specific scents by hiding a treat in a scent container.

Interactive feeding: Instead of feeding your dog in a bowl, try hiding food in different locations around the house and encourage them to find it.

Memory games

Teach your dog to remember the locations of different objects and retrieve them on command.

Sure, here are a few examples of memory games for dogs along with instructions:

The Shell Game

The Shell Game is a classic memory game that can be easily adapted for dogs. This game stimulates a dog's cognitive skills as they have to use their memory to remember which cup has the treat and then use their problem-solving skills to figure out which cup to choose. Here's how to play:

- Gather three plastic cups and place a treat under one of them.
- Shuffle the cups around so that the dog can't see which one has the treat.

- Encourage the dog to choose the correct cup by pointing at it or using a verbal cue.
- If the dog chooses the correct cup, they get the treat!

The Muffin Tin Game

The Muffin Tin Game is another fun memory game for dogs that can be easily set up with materials you may already have at home. This game stimulates a dog's sense of smell and memory as they have to remember which cups have treats and use their sense of smell to find them.

Here's how to play:

- Take a muffin tin and place a treat in a few of the cups.
- Cover each treat with a tennis ball or another similar-sized object.
- Encourage the dog to find the treats by using their nose to move the objects out of the way.

The Treasure Hunt Game

The treasure hunt game stimulates a dog's natural instincts to sniff out and search for food or toys. It also challenges their memory and problem-solving skills as they have to remember where the treasures are hidden.

- Hide treats or toys in different areas of the house or backyard.
- Encourage your dog to find the hidden treasures by giving them

verbal cues or pointing in the right direction.
- Once your dog has found all the treasures, reward them with praise or extra treats.

Name recognition

The Name Recognition exercise stimulates a dog's cognitive abilities by requiring them to learn and remember the names of different people or pets in their household. It also improves their focus, attention, and impulse control. This exercise is particularly helpful for dogs who need to learn to differentiate between different family members or pets and respond to their names. Additionally, practicing name recognition can strengthen the bond between the dog and their human family members by encouraging communication and positive reinforcement.

- Start by teaching your dog to recognize their own name. Choose a quiet and distraction-free area to train your dog.
- Say your dog's name in a clear and upbeat tone of voice, and immediately give them a treat or a toy as a reward.
- Repeat this exercise several times a day until your dog consistently looks at you or comes to you when you say their name.
- Once your dog has mastered their own name, you can start teaching them to recognize the names of other people or pets in the household.
- Repeat the same exercise as above, but use the names of other people or pets in the household instead of your dog's name.
- Gradually increase the difficulty of the exercise by introducing more names or adding distractions to the environment.

Mental exercise is a crucial part of keeping your dog healthy and happy. It not only stimulates their cognitive abilities but also provides a sense of mental satisfaction that is just as important as physical exercise. By incorporating mental exercise into your dog's routine, you can keep them engaged, challenged, and fulfilled. Try out the examples provided in this chapter and see the difference it can make for your furry friend!

16

Conclusion

Congratulations, you have reached the end of this training bible for dogs! Throughout this book, you have learned a variety of training techniques to help your furry friend become a well-behaved and happy member of your family.

You have learned the importance of positive reinforcement and how to use it effectively to train your dog. You have learned how to teach basic commands such as "sit," "stay," and "come," as well as advanced commands such as "heel" and "off-leash training." You have also learned about socialization training and agility training, both of which can help your dog to develop confidence and coordination.

By following these training techniques, you will not only improve your dog's behavior but also strengthen your relationship with your pet. Consistency, patience, and love are the keys to success in dog training.

If you are a puppy owner, remember that it is never too early to start training your dog. The earlier you begin, the easier it will be to teach your puppy good behavior habits. Make training fun and positive, and your puppy will be eager to learn and please you.

Key Takeaways

- Use positive reinforcement to train your dog
- Consistency and patience are essential for successful training
- Start training your dog as early as possible
- Basic commands are the foundation of good behavior
- Advanced training techniques can help your dog to develop confidence and coordination
- Grooming is an important part of your dog's care routine
- Having a dog as a life companion can bring immeasurable joy and love into our lives. They provide us with unconditional love, loyalty, and companionship that can enrich our lives in countless ways.
- Dogs have a unique ability to lift our spirits and provide comfort during difficult times. They are always there to greet us with a wagging tail and a happy face, which can help reduce our stress levels and bring a smile to our faces.

Additionally, dogs can help us stay active and lead healthier lives. Taking them for walks, playing fetch, and engaging in other physical activities not only benefit our dogs, but also provide us with much-needed exercise and fresh air.

Dogs can also improve our social lives. Whether we're walking our dogs in the park or attending obedience classes, we have the opportunity to meet and connect with other dog owners who share our love and passion for dogs.

Finally, owning a dog can teach us valuable life lessons such as responsibility, patience, and compassion. We learn to care for another living being and develop a deep sense of empathy and understanding. By nurturing the bond between you and your furry friend, you can create a lifelong partnership that is full of love and happiness

17

FAQ

Q: What is the most appropriate age to start training a dog?

A: It's best to start training your dog as soon as you bring them home with you, which is usually between 8 and 12 weeks old. At this age, they are most receptive to learning and are still developing their personality and habits.

Q: How much time does it normally take to train a dog?

A: The time it takes to train a dog varies depending on the dog's breed, age, and temperament, as well as the complexity of the training. Basic obedience training can take a few weeks to a few months, while more advanced training can take a few months to a year or more.

Q: What is positive reinforcement, and why is it an important training method for dogs?

A: Positive reinforcement is a training method that rewards your dog for good behavior. This can be done by using treats, toys, praise, or anything else your dog enjoys. The idea behind positive reinforcement is to encourage your dog to repeat good behaviors by associating them with positive outcomes. This method is important because it is gentle and effective, and helps to build a strong bond between you and your dog.

Q: How to teach dogs to stop barking excessively?

A: Excessive barking can be a frustrating problem for dog owners, but it can be addressed with training. The first step is to identify why your dog is barking, which may include boredom, anxiety, or a desire for attention. Once you know the cause, you can work on teaching your dog an alternative behavior, such as going to their bed or crate, when they feel the urge to bark. You can also use positive reinforcement to reward your dog for quiet behavior, and desensitization techniques to help them get used to the triggers that cause them to bark excessively.

Q: What are some commonly made mistakes to avoid when training a dog?

A: One of the most common mistakes dog owners make is expecting too much too soon from their dog. It's important to remember that training takes time and patience, and that your dog will learn at their own pace. Another mistake is being inconsistent with your training methods, which can confuse your dog and make it harder for them to learn. Finally, it's important to avoid using punishment or physical force as a training method, as this can damage your relationship with your dog and cause them to become fearful or aggressive.

Q: How can I socialize my dog with other dogs and people?

A: Socialization is an important part of training for dogs, as it helps them learn how to interact with other people and dogs in a positive and confident way. The best way to socialize your dog is to expose them to a variety of different situations, people, and dogs in a controlled and positive way. This can include taking them on walks in busy areas, introducing them to new dogs one at a time, and giving them plenty of positive reinforcement when they behave well in social situations.

Q: What should I do if my dog shows signs of aggression?

A: Aggression is a serious problem in dogs and should be addressed with professional help. If your dog shows signs of aggression, like growling, biting, or lunging, it's important to seek the advice of a certified dog trainer or behaviorist. They can help you identify the cause of the aggression and come up with a training plan to address the problem. In some cases, medication may also be required to help your dog manage their aggression.

Q: How do I teach my dog to walk on a leash without pulling?

A: Leash pulling is a common problem for dog owners, but it can be addressed with training. The first step is to use a properly fitted harness or collar that doesn't cause discomfort or pain to your dog. Next, start training your dog in a low-distraction environment, such as your backyard, using positive reinforcement to reward them for walking calmly beside you. As your dog becomes more comfortable, gradually increase the level of distraction and distance of your walks. Consistency is key, and it's important to reward your dog every time they walk without pulling.

Q: How do I teach my dog to come when called?

A: Teaching your dog to come when called is an important part of basic obedience training. Start by using a specific command, such as "come," and calling your dog to you in a low-distraction environment. When they come to you, reward them with praise, treats, or a toy.

Q: How do I prevent my dog from chewing on furniture and other household items?

A: Dogs often chew on household items out of boredom or anxiety. To prevent this behavior, provide your dog with plenty of toys and chew treats, and make sure they get enough exercise and mental stimulation. You can also use bitter sprays or deterrents on furniture and other items to make them less appealing to your dog.

Q: How can I teach and show my dog how to play fetch?

A: Teaching your dog to play fetch can be a fun and rewarding way to bond with them. Start by using a toy that your dog likes, such as a ball or Frisbee, and throwing it a short distance. When your dog brings it back, reward them with praise, treats, or another throw. Repeat this process, gradually increasing the distance of your throws and the complexity of the game.

Q: How can I train my puppy to stay calm during thunderstorms?

A: Thunderstorms can be a source of anxiety for dogs, but there are ways to help them stay calm. You can create a safe space for your puppy, such as a crate or a designated room, and provide them with calming music or a thunder shirt. It's also important to remain calm yourself and not reinforce your dog's anxiety by giving them too much attention. Gradual desensitization can also help, by exposing your dog to the sound of thunder and rewarding them for staying calm.